Under The Hours

Praise for Barbara Cully's previous books:

Desire Reclining (2003): When Carolyn Forché chose Barbara Cully's first book, *The New Intimacy*, for the National Poetry Series, she wrote that Cully "is, in her transgressive, ruptured, and disjunctive poetics, seeking *a language for the unspeakable shame of the world*...[and] locates her hope in a present glimmering with futurity." Cully's new collection...is suffused with the same wit, compassion, and conscience that have distinguished her previous work.
—Penguin Books

That Place Where (Kore Press, 2011): Here is a consummate poet at the height of her interrogation of language, philosophy, and philology. Barbara Cully is a poet's poet. She speaks passionately without ambition, fanfare, or guile.
—Jane Miller

A Place Where One (Green Linden Press, 2017): "To enter this book is to walk along during a shoreline meditation. We sift through the layers and find that all is change. This is its power: the mind cuts the veil of conceptual thought to the impermanence that is shared.
—Beth Alvarado

Also by Barbara Cully

Back Apart (2021)

A Place Where One (2017)

That Place Where (2011)

Desire Reclining (2003)

Shoreline Series (1997)

The New Intimacy (1997)

Under The Hours

Barbara Cully

JACKLEG PRESS

Acknowledgments

I gratefully acknowledge the editors of the following publications in which some of these poems first appeared: *Arizona Highways* (excerpt of "Your Exile, My--" titled "Pusch Ridge"); *Category* ("Song"); *CUE: A Journal of Prose Poetry* ("Under the Hours"); *Eleven Eleven* ("Glorietta Canyon," and "Tabulation"); *Softblow* (excerpts of "Your Exile, My--"); *Sonora Review* ("Spikes of/*Espigas de*"); and *Venus Salon* (excerpts of "Your Exile, My--").

Many thanks to Jennifer Harris of JackLeg Press for her request of this book and for her inspired design and creation of it. *Mil gracias* to Bruce and Marsha Boston for years of inspiration. Endless gratitude to my readers Beth Alvarado, Jacqueline Cully, Jesse Seldess, Boyer Rickel, and Kim Westerman who cheered these poems on. The full names of those I dedicate this book to, with love, are: Boyer Rickel, Morgan Lucas Schuldt, and Victoria Garza.

For more information on this book or to order, visit www.jacklegpress.org

Published by

JackLeg Press
Washington, DC

© 2021 Barbara Cully
First edition, 2012
All rights reserved.
Printed in the United States of America.

ISBN: 978-1-7373307-1-4

No part of this work may be reproduced or utilized in any form or by any means, electronic or mechanical, including photocopying, microfilm, and recording, or by any information storage and retrieval system, without permission in writing from the publisher.

Library of Congress Cataloging-in-Publication Data

for Boyer, Morgan, & Victoria

Because we waltzed
because beneath
motionless sky.

Contents

Under the Hours

Song	1
Glorietta Canyon	3
Under the Hours	4
[Untitled]	7
(Immersion)	8
Song	9
Blue Heron	10
Every Waking Hour	11
Sea Level	13
Imperial Dune	14
The Wave Crest	15
Monsoon	16
Tidal	17
Wing Shining Days	18
Song	19
Tabulation	20
Song	21
Threshold	22
Suppose the Air	24

Your Exile, My—

By the way we give ourselves to half the world,	27
Many sunsets, and one of them a little brutal,	28
Fireworks on the beach—or "in the cards"?	29
Remote in this desert, I was with you	30
Do you hear it too?	31
(My sister came as an apparition in her uniform,	32
The long and the short	33
Two Chilean mesquites tremble	34
If confronting the wall, you choose	35
Waiting? (The day is finished.)	36
The hours	37
You wake with a convulsive start,	38
Glide forward in the dark, my skiff, my keel,	39
(Aria of want sounding):	40
At dawn,	41
The big-horned sheep in the Catalinas	42
The lavender-washed sky;	43
With shears do I cut away a face?	44
The succulent that spreads its rose	45
...so be it. Sounds of buses	46

Spikes of (Espigas de)

Yellow, yellow—the color the sun	*49*
So shall you see—	*50*
It is one of the first mornings,	*51*
The urban-scape is filled with whatevers,	*53*
This sand is this sand and it is cold,	*54*
The dead's eyes been spoken.	*55*
The day has come and the meek,	*56*
The addicted legion sleep on the beach	*57*
Hey, poke that guy with the sack over	*58*
The exotic and the colorful ringed planet Saturn	*59*
A small coterie of animals drawn to look	*60*
Notes	*61*
About the Author	*62*

Under the Hours

"It rained last night. The dead came down with the rain."
"You mean their voices?"
"Yes, of course, their voices."

—Tennessee Williams, *Memoirs*

Song

There is no fixed form to yoke the carving hand
There is no carving hand advancing for you

There is silence and all the chords muted
There is the water lily on its circular pad

And there is you—
(Black hour gone) on the opposite bank turning

    *

The pressure upon the organ between the barriers before
    the altar where beauty once appeared—

And heart—how full is the half we caress and caress?

    *

Slowly and silently we get on with the shaping and naming
    that comes like a wheel
Slowly and silently we construct the pavilion of brightness
    past

So much wind to make the stillness enormous
So many door handles and hinges to make the stillness a
    pavilion

Our song will go with the shouting
Our shouting with the drums and heads
                      of the severe saints in the rain

A bit tired of ourselves and our own sort of singing
We'll walk the many steps
      to a wooden horse or a boat in the waves

Glorietta Canyon

In the shadow shadowless in the dream in the quiet
in the shadow shadowless in the sunset.

The yellow cholla aglow and the moon in the motion
    motionless
with her sister and the dead one's bones pared into
    sandstone.

Each sacred body part laid like research on the bed—
each a notice of the days clicking while the saints and the
    heels saunter by.

All equally welcome, we welcome the fluids that tell us the
    direction in which to—
(I mean, it is necessary to decipher the direction rain would
    take in the snow.)

Calm now—the world assembles itself, and we do not
    kneel at its feet in greeting.
Departed with a gesture of thanks and a tentative
    blessing—Departed with a face
open and bare.

Weightless, the torrential grief descending.

Under the Hours

I had a bag of free flowers fallen from a flower cart. You were there, next to me in the garden where I almost embraced you in front of the participants. Brazen orange amid bursts of violet disorganized: The western twilight like cats and bamboo radiant and untameable. This end of day become a living rule; become our decision to accept the wet silence of the mouth—mouths—of night—to come.

You were there as those with pointed hats and the rest of the departing mountains changed face next to the distant barracks. About face/faces there is much to remember into the yellowing dusk. Oh, I do not mean to mix your tea leaves with my yarrow stalks; I mean to tell you about disbelieved years and faucets running open, about the infants and dogs that gnawed at me face down on my pillows.

Waking up inside the sound of steadfast waves, finally enough time to practice growing old, older. First a hand suspended in green air descending then the body, hoping, delicate and rowing. Soon the desert creek (in memory) as water scrubbing. Those enormous boulders rounded gray and cascading into immaculate flowers fading. There you have it foot-trampled god how beautiful.

Don't mistake me now for a small girl in someone's arms pretending to read. Mistake me for a secret case in your room under the chiaroscuro of paper rising like estuary grasses in flames. Study me, and when I am tested, forgive me or rate me higher than I deserve. After this I promise dinner and a collision of days like tongues clucked sweetly under the hours.

In the end mathematics will treat us more kindly than the laws of physics with their cheerful teeth and prescient sense of decay. But as we rock and rest, as we sip and weep, tell the one about the (Catholic) father and the daughter; tell the one about the grandma and the far-flung turtles; tell the one about the maimed dog that lasted and the women who wanted to—fixing their hats precisely as they did before the fair.

Fine then, flourish. Flourish and take several souvenirs. Buy Italian, eat Greek and put those roses in something pretty before lunch cools beyond repair. Spring now, or summer, as it is, like afternoon, laid out for the taking in the yard.

[Untitled]

You were saying, no, singing, and I was going off
    somewhere.

You, stretched along the steady forest humus, and I a pale
cherry blossom going off somewhere.

        So quickly the wind cannot be observed—
        When morning begins unrolling into—

When we slide, still desiring, into the part of the garment
    that covers all or part of the
head and face,

do not be afraid. What comes comes in place of one who
has closed her eyes like a mountain,

its filling waters boulder gray and green.

More than once we have heard at noon first a bray and
    then a bleat and cackle
cawing out the story of the tiny world.

        Noisily day and night
        from the mouth and full of joy.

(Immersion)

Shapes of paper shifting and floating over the sea wall like
    leaves
A bit of shadow amid the air that rises moist between the
    vine and eaves

What you have said you have said more than a hundred
    times
I heard you but once like an emerald star at the waterline
    suddenly

The stillness of dusk in the orb that floats
The jellyfish-surge of blood in the arm that subsides

        The hum on the tongue but the lungs holding
        The salt in the wave against the teeth parting

Song

What you knew of me we carried until what we knew of
 you became a song of summer

The thick, dark, rain-saturated grass

Nearby lay the phantom of a years-old conversation, always
 naked, always face up

In the mustard bristle of the vacant field

Are we now among those who breathe the sweet gusts
 between the buildings?

Thought is not evening; I walk and talk slowly, my
 shoulders slumping

Until as my eyelids rise, you abruptly offer yourself seaside
 while no one is looking

Soon enough, brightly clad bathers and their children
 running

If I were the one they were chasing, if I were a pigeon or
 dragonfly who—

Here in the water against the peak of the waves

You rest in the damp steeple of the eaves

Blue Heron

Birds listen, intently silent. How hot it is.

Only a guinea hen—two, scratching.

In the morning scorch of sun the hand remembers:

The hand held out far from the body—to be
 photographed?—

To be considered and greeted years from now—

A day like any other day.

I intend to listen intently, to say two things, to take my
 leave,

My hands outstretched—the last of friends—the first of
 friends—to say with thanks

Goodbye to—Look here—your face among the lines of my
 heart—

My destiny of destinies, wafting gleefully, rises turning
 without end.

Every Waking Hour

What you have sung, said

Risen now, against my rootedness

                                            my torment
                    oh my mouth
                                      against the boulders

Vein dry leg   walked off alone

                              you as maybe waft
                              where I am not

                                    curve of the world
                                    maybe mist

Here my arm
            arid wind

                    succulent bud-studded unfurled
            cliff—broken sky

              ocean break wave break shore break
      wind

Where you—

                              you—descend

Desert algae

   upon   across   beside   at noon   furrowed

Sea Level

wildfires—we

revere the birds who toss their hearts

over billowy horns

Imperial Dune

even a mouse submerged in sleep

is hard at work—do you hear me?

(I have come)

The Wave Crest

what you have said to me

over, like a town or city

half unwalled

Monsoon

not far, in a half bowl

see them—

creatures sweet

Tidal

now from the balcony

broken silhouette of riders'

hooves and bells

Wing Shining Days

Wing shining days inside the lull tide,
unseen days.

A congregation of pelicans dives, busy with the feast,
swallowing the organs of duration.

When what we love (beloved) dives, asks to be hollowed,
remains to be seen,

buildings and dunes undulate through the flames,
a shroud of swallows intent on returning.

When you set out—
a tiny slip for the one who sails

(sea foam perpetual—
a thought long believing).

Evening came, drifting.
You too, broken lily, lifted—

letting
whatever vapors held you let you go.

Song

You—descend,
while I with rain from my dark veranda fall.
Sunlit, pale, drunk with noon—

Vague, tender mountain, lunar hue
above ocean water, no—
remote city—now no road—

Late, later—a crowd of night birds mocks
eternal sleep.
In the lull-tide of squid and foam,

what you have said
mimes a rain choir—voices
we have lived.

Tabulation

The dictionary
as a record of its transformed materials—
catalogued—as the contents of a beach house
borrowed.

The morning tide—so far back—
the shoreline delays itself in a pause before noon.
(Here you—
you descend.)

What you have said—dispelled
with the earthen heat—
absent now
in the day's dusk reckoning.

Song

The longer one waited
the more it brings us again—

                                        pulse in your ears,
                              dropped to my knees,

night wind
in the tide
between the earth and its amber.

                                And I, not far, been spoken.

The day's stalk trembled.
Questions remain   full of houses?
A heart, nowhere in motion—

      Memory ceasing
      the stroke that severs,

      anyhow—wavers,
      when you—you ascend.

Threshold

The ripple of mica imprinted in wet sand left of the jetty
and north of Calafia—
where mounds of kelp and the minus-tide conjure a
peninsula nearing nightfall.

All the cloud strokes illuminated: Now a western orb
    speaks to the orient—its fuchsias,
its yellows.

Out of the order, the universal. And a recognition that the
breath cuts off mid-sentence in a heat belt while the body
continues to rise.

What we have adheres to the governing powers: Irresolute
    flames and cumulus. Micro-
organized cliff walls of mortar and wire.

At the first drink of the day—what I have wished for you:
    the flaw in the net that binds.
Two or three palms wave and clap the effort at the curved
end of the drive.

At the curved end of the drive, not a garden but a reliquary.
    After the dirt and stones,
after the torqued hands and limbs—

The wind in the orchard carries back the tidal, surge of life.

Suppose the Air

excluding none of its colors now at the tide.
Now that a low-slung blue
huddles beyond a dark veranda wall,

the muddled sea of sky changes.
Suppose the air
asleep on its back in the marsh of grasses

violet again amid the celery stalks of summer.
What colors? Egret exceeding the indigo horizon.
What color? Egret conceding to dusk.

Your Exile, My—

By the way we give ourselves to half the world,
the heart knows its compatriot.
Within its chambers, a rough sea or effulgence

on the eve of departure
small chance amid the boulders
as the pulse begins to trill.

If I or my sister—if you or your mother,
if I could but never—give up this storm
for our dinner—

The solace of ripe oranges,
or a bloody fisher in an apron,
the solace of a doubt cast darkly.

Every dog bark a pistol,
unto the salt breeze its whistle,
the moon either huge or a cloud among the wharves.

Sitting on *the words* (small craft amid the shallows)
beyond all decision
always I must lose you again

Many sunsets, and one of them a little brutal,
dusk falling, creek flaming
like a banner down the wash.

From the sidelines,
my heart like estuary grass
(a little brittle) calls you back.

A voice like straw quaking.
Thunderous marriage deafening
like a wounded dragon falling.

Fireworks on the beach—or "in the cards"?
Children erupting like ballerinas in the sand.

A few miles north our country
readies for war.

In my sickbed you administer.
At the sink I expire.

The day you hit the tiles crying,
I was awake and you—solid gone.

Remote in this desert, I was with you
when your father went into his death bed and returned.

What message for us from him in that
mechanical delirium and gratefulness?

A difficult future we have been spared for this:
I know you and you know me from the pain of today.

The hours will bend back on themselves,
and we'll walk the beach you imagined for us in old age.

My old age, coming first, searching your eyes,
as your youth, lingering, shielded mine.

Do you hear it too?

The train as it hollers through the barrio—
hooting, not dancing
like our guinea hens.

How cold it is.
Under the cement of the freeway,
the homeless swaying and coughing.

(Could they possibly be right?)
Bowing faces in the dark,
the way not to say goodbye.

(My sister came as an apparition in her uniform,
dragging her two Pekingese on a leash):

You were there—next to me in the garden, picking
our ripened oranges.

I had almost cremated our scrap of images—dazzling,
a yellow home vaporized in one hundred degrees and
wafting.

In the adobe alcove, *la Virgen*:
her visage gray and bleached but not distorted.

I asked the roses about this thing cutting me off
from every trace of you—then

I asked you.

The long and the short
ascending and descending

sequence between two swallows' nests:
What will ease the distance if not

the ache and the arc of you?
My limbs brought back to the river

(dry though it is)
by my own heart's cycling.

If the eucalyptus trees shedding their perfume
above the powdered earth

signify a truce,
the roiling monsoon of you

threatens to consume it.

Two Chilean mesquites tremble
over a wall made splendid rose
by the dawn.

The Madonna's face, worried by erosion, made
confident and blind by the sunlight.
Two Meyer lemons aglow.

These three signs, as children walk
neatly in procession into the park.
Sweet conversation in the rustle

dusting up from their shoes:
Sun-still glitter of this life
we had made.

If confronting the wall, you choose
another shape: all of them squares
or creek stones.

If with your back to the great sail of dust on the wind:
the moon with its clock face, fainter
than your heart.

If beyond the rock stubble, a green
lizard like a dart, staid
in the sunflash of the driest clearing:

(What then?)
Without its sounds
time signifies nothing.

Waiting? (The day is finished.)
Why you are—torch-like, the skyline's
flash of lightning against the cloud.

The thumbnail moon risen.
Its one tip reaching with Venus
for the sun.

Lazy with my rake, I gather
the day's words—beaten,
to cover you.

Pine tree, why
does—startled by a breeze—
nothing end?

The hours
as a spirit scattering
your voice on finches' wings in the air.

I will always know you.
Your design is always there.
We do not feed on the accidental blessing:

do, re, mi—
but scatter—(*sol, á*)
into each new season.

God from the machine—
hidden or seen, comes back happy
to portend of other things.

You wake with a convulsive start,
and I wipe the spider remnants
from your hair.

You are not here.
(You crossed the highest clouds.)
Noon: and the black shadow of the meadow lark
accruing against the square.

...Other shadows building in the alley
and I know and do not know
the sun torn by cyclones and the ice—

Glide forward in the dark, my skiff, my keel,
one evening out of many.

The moonlit splendor of polished stones and poppies on
    the bank:
mounds of eels and rigging far behind you.

(A blue-black tangle in the water, deeper still.)
A fisher as a butcher in an apron and our song, red

as the doors that close close behind you.
Joined so intently.

(Aria of want sounding):

Is it a suite for unaccompanied cello
or a hell's-night-out player piano
coming in for the kill as it mounts and trills?

(Beneath water, salt in my mouth,
your storm in me bellowing,
is it rain or dust roiling?)

What you once woke in me
wakes in me—destroying the bellflower
and toppling the bougainvillea.

At dawn,
the screech of the train
speeding through downtown
tells the story of the child trapped in the tunnel,
crying out but lit by the certainty of rescue.

At dusk, when the tomato worm
eating through the yard
redoubles its efforts,
the footsteps of the poem needles closer:
"At dawn and at dusk"—"the train and the worm"—
even these become mined,
indelibly connected,
woven together with our song.

The big-horned sheep in the Catalinas
repeating their footholds from cliff to cliff

have no days more angled nor sharper
than the crevice, serpentine, between us.

No screech of an owl, no talons prying us apart—
the unrelenting blue sky building.

In air so dry the solar heat hurts right through it,
a spider's rope leads me to the trail crest where

I do not leave a mark.

The lavender-washed sky;
daylight erased in a *woosh*;

the desert dove last to try its wings tonight
in a mountain-choked puddle of sun.

Ochre rays aloft.
Their slow weave

through the *palo verdes*—gnarled
among the houses, emitting a little warmth—

where the distant freeway hums
in the pastel hour of the urban barrio.

                        One death
and another shrine is erected—another saint
the color of slate

poised to deliver
breath-thin hopes on flaming hooves.

With shears do I cut away a face?
The last curve in the about-to-be buried poem,
the last vestige of a backward-glancing look
at a desert garden enclosed forever?

Tonight a frost descends...so I'll cover the bougainvillea.
At the base of the scorched lemon,
the shells of my far off beach surface
in the mud of every November.

The succulent that spreads its rose
disks—winter or spring;
the path where walkers hover
on night's dark current—tugging
their leashed jackals: briefly,
the dogs and owners breathless
and free of home.

Tonight there is much
that you might recognize:
a yellow house where tomatoes flare and burn
and a violet sun refuses to fade.
Beyond our eyes, shielded now,
two or more ribbons of smoke
spiral and cross,
                        the gust passes.

...so be it. Sounds of buses
mingled with the bees
needling the penstemon.

                        Two birds
painted on a split of eucalyptus bark
dance brightly in the sunset.

Even the preserved tarantula
in its domed stasis of resin
does its duty shining:

steadfast,
the loose stack of pages
in a life that seems so vast.

Spikes of (*Espigas de*)

This planet, carpet thousands of years old,
shall flourish but it does not accept death nor repose.

—Pablo Neruda, "2000"

Yellow, yellow—the color the sun
        does not wear,
borne up to me via the steps
        by a dog.
Stone steps higher
        than waves resounding.
Stone of the earth-house black
        dismantled, while this
house, corridor of moistened windows,
        stands.

So shall you see—

(Who if)

How can one

on the—

on the—

as soon as

let us simply

espiga, espiga!

Do you see—hushed and with

a shamed swallow—

       your century gorged—burst and rotted

       in so many yokel graves—

It is one of the first mornings,
        and I think I smell our trash.
Dawn of the first day running,
        our garbage ripe, aloft.

The gill and the gaze, the soft web
        of the parrot-fish who gave—
Spinach and the beer at the bottom,
        sand and the glow of chicken fat,
        final along the rim.

        The women, the dead and the men and the
materials (used up)—
            of the last decades
            have asked to speak—And the mountains
            and the oceans of the ravenous invasions.
        But how we have strayed, lady.

No, it is not the first morning,
        dawn-green resplendent of the fourth or fifth.

Sanderlings at the shore and running.

Thank god
       that president, with his cheerfulness,
          finally vanished.

Praised be
       the youth clearing his lungs.

Each day, a sandwich
       come out to greet us.
       (In your beach chair.)

Each day, the burst of tides
       and dirt and glass.

The urban-scape is filled with whatevers,
> unaccounted for ruptures and gain.

What does that paper say the vanquished feel?

Yet we must—

lolling—our tongues in our mouths,
> cut this or that chin angle
> next to this or that horror.

What the captive feel

we ask.

When the beheaded speak,

we turn.

This sand is this sand and it is cold,
> that is certain.

I dragged a shovel behind me,
> of that there can be no doubt.

The major high tide and the quarter moon
> will converge at six-thirty this evening.

The surreptitious transference of power
> will have taken place

while today is today and yesterday has passed.

The dead's eyes been spoken.
        Near or on or in the forest maw.

The burst abdomen of hope in the socket,
        the gel that forms
        when the last domestic cat returns.

Mother wake me,
        I have drunk too much of the ointment
        our leaders pour.

The day has come and the meek,
        wary of their inheritance,
        approximate a hungry cue.

There, far behind—your parents.
        There—cousins all,
        hailing you.

The addicted legion sleep on the beach
> while the pyramids and the Buddhas
> are prepared for destruction
> over eons
> pane by pane and stone by stone.

A bent bowl for the vomit of the children
> in the government-sanctioned
> house of the lord.

Hey, poke that guy with the sack over
> his head—like all the rest,
> > he wants to be abducted and probed.

That's a box cutter in his pocket,
> or he is enjoying the show.

In his dreams, the director booms—dressed in burka and heels,
> overwhelming the conversation
> with all that no longer abides.

Upon your own return to the action,
that place where
quietly closing the door.

The exotic and the colorful ringed planet Saturn
      ... on Wednesday evening
      over the next four years ...

The frigid surface of Titan,
        the only moon in the solar system
        with the dense chemical possibility

of returning to the
of washing up to
of breaking ever-after.

So many years and days in bundles
        —used by guerrillas for surveillance of the outpost
        —aimed with a degree of accuracy
        —fall hollowly.

A small coterie of animals drawn to look
        like cats or pigs advancing blithely
        over an expanse of tile.

As news of the take-over spread.

From now on your parents will be
        two splits of wood you carry
        under each arm
        the length of the beach toward the fire.

Notes

"Gorietta Canyon" is for my sister Jacqueline Cully and for Kenton Kitterman.

"Blue Heron": The opening lines owe a debt to Aleksander Wat's "Songs of a Wanderer," translated from the Polish by Czeslaw Milosz and Leonard Nathan.

"Threshold": In part, the poem echoes and answers Eugenio Montale's "In Limine" ("On the Threshold"). The last line is Montale's.

"Suppose the Air" draws from Rafael Alberti's "Going Back through Color."

"Your Exile, My—" is after Eugenio Montale's "Mottetti: Poems of Love" in *Le Occasioni*.

"Spikes of (*Espigas de*)": The title and some lines echo Pablo Neruda's poem "2000."

About the Author

Barbara Cully is the author of two poetry collections from Penguin Books: *Desire Reclining* and *The New Intimacy*, which won the National Poetry Series Award, and two collections from Kore Press: *Shoreline Series* and *That Place Where*. In addition, she has published *Under the Hours* and *Back Apart* (Jackleg Press) and *A Place Where One* (Green Linden Press). She is co-editor of two writing textbooks *Writing as Revision* and *Entry Points* (Pearson). She taught for many years in the Department of English and Honors College at the University of Arizona, has been a guest writer at the Prague Summer Writing Program, and was recently awarded the title Distinguished Adjunct Professor by Golden Gate University, San Francisco. She was born in and grew up in San Diego, California.

Under the Hours. Barbara Cully

Hallucinogenesis. D.C. Gonzales-Prieto

Trapline. Caroline Goodwin

This is How I Dream It. Jennifer Harris

Men in Correspondence. Meagan Lehr

Observations of an Orchestrated Catastrophe. Jenny Magnus

when i am yes. cin salach

Two Thieves and a Liar. Neil de la Flor, Maureen Seaton, and Kristine Snodgrass

Genetics. Maureen Seaton

Undersea. Maureen Seaton

Rank. Kristine Snodgrass

The War on Pants. Kristine Snodgrass

jacklegpress.org

www.ingramcontent.com/pod-product-compliance
Lightning Source LLC
Chambersburg PA
CBHW020914080526
44589CB00011B/589